You Press 'Enter' on the Browser

What happens when..., Volume 1

Dustin W. Morris

Published by Dustin W. Morris, 2025.

YOU PRESS 'ENTER' ON THE BROWSER

First edition. January 8, 2025.

ISBN: 979-8230010845

Written by Dustin W. Morris.

Table of Contents

Thank you to my family, Catherine, Zachary, Wesley, Bonnie, Brayeden, Grayeson, and RayeLaia.

I
The Hardware

"Software gets slower faster than hardware gets faster."

– Niklaus Wirth

And the magic begins, when we press the "enter" key.

The keyboard consists of the following critical components:

- domed key sheet
- top conductive sheet
- middle spacer sheet
- bottom conductive sheet
- circuit card

The top sheet has twelve conductive traces and the bottom sheet has eleven conductive traces printed on it (11*12 = 132 keys). The middle sheet separates the top and bottom conductive sheets so that when a key is press they make contact. The circuit card provides 3 volts of power to the bottom sheet. When a key is pressed, the rubber domed key sheet presses the top sheet between the spacer sheet and makes contact to the 3 volts on the bottom sheet. The circuit is complete and the power flows to the microprocessor on the circuit card of the keyboard.[3]

For example, when "R" is pressed the bottom sheet trace 3 applies voltage to the top sheet trace 2. Every 65 ms, one of the bottom sheet traces is turned off. The microprocessor will see a pulsing every 65 ms on the key the trace that is pushed. The correlation between the bottom

bottom sheet

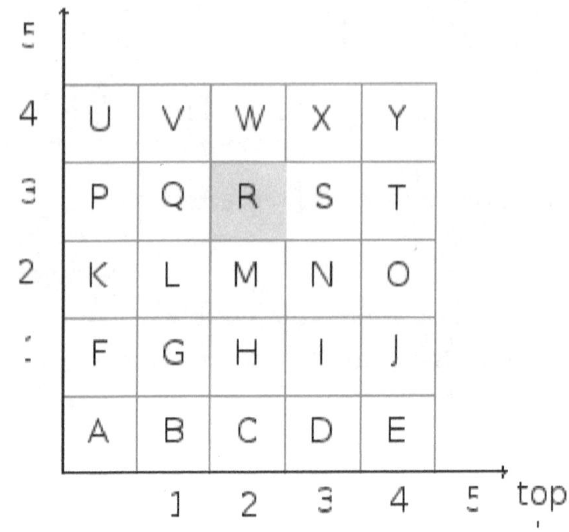

Figure I.1: Keyboard Matrix

circuit pulse and the top circuit pulse uniquely identify the key that is pressed.

The keyboard's microprocessor converts the signal to a scan code that the computer's keyboard controller understands.

In modern computers, the keyboard controller is integrated with the USB (Universal Serial Bus) controller. The purpose of the keyboard controller is to raise a keyboard interrupt to allow the CPU (central processing unit) to handle the input. The exact key is binary encoded in the keyboard buffer memory until it is processed by the CPU.[5]

The USB controller is based on a host/worker architecture capable of supporting 127 devices. When a new device, such as the keyboard, is connected, the host assigns a unique address to the device and queries it for information such as device type, manufacturer, and supported configurations. The host loads the appropriate driver for the device, allowing it to communicate with the operating system and applications. USB devices support different types of data transfer such as isochronous for audio and video streaming, bulk transfer for file transfers, and interrupt transfers for time-critical data transfers such as keyboard and mouse inputs. Similar to other networks described in the networking chapter, data is transferred in packets on USB lines that include the device address, endpoint number, error-checking information, and the data payload.

II
The Operating System

"Operating systems are like underwear – Nobody really wants to look at them."

– Bill Joy

And now the OS (operating system) must deal with the interruption. The OS checks if any modifier keys such as "Shift", "Ctrl", or "Alt" are pressed. The OS then places the keyboard event which includes the generated characteror function(if a modifier was found) in the OS's event queue. The operating system then dispatches the keyboard event to the active application. In this case, the browser is the active application.

In the Linux operating system, **/dev/input/eventX** where X is an integer assigned to an input device represent events from various inputs, including keyboards. The **/dev/tty** filer epresents the terminal interface. The **/etc/default/keyboard** file contains the default keyboard layout and settings for the system. The **/etc/inputrc** file contains configuration settings for the Readline library, which handles keyboard input for command-line interfaces. The **hid-generic** kernel module handles generic Human Interface Devices. The **usbhid** kernel module handles USB Human Interface Devices. The **libinput** library provides a unified input device handling for Wayland and X11. The **evdev** library provides an interface for handling input events from device files in **/dev/input/**.

The Windows operating system consists of several DLLs (dynamic list libraries) that handle keyboard inputs. The **kbdclass.sys** is a kernel mode[1]driver that manages keyboard input at a low level. It processes the scan codes from the keyboard and passes them to the appropriate higher-level components. The **user32.dll** is responsible for handling user input, including keyboard and mouse events. It provides functions for managing windows, handling messages, and processing input. The

win32k.sys is a kernel-mode driver that handles low-level input processing, including keyboard and mouse events. It works closely with **user32.dll** to manage input and windowing. The **hid.dll** is part of the Human Interface Device (HID) subsystem and is responsible for handling input from various HID devices, including keyboards.

The driver converts the scan code which is device independent to a virtual-key code which is OS dependent. The keyboard creates a message which goes into Windows system queue. A system message is generated which goes into the thread message queue. When the thread is active via the thread message loop, the input goes into the windows procedure. [4]

One of the many tasks of the operating system does is handle different keyboard layouts. The scan codes are translated differently for different keyboard layouts. In addition, the operating system must handle different languages. The map between the scan code and the virtual-key is all handled by the operating system and the device driver software.

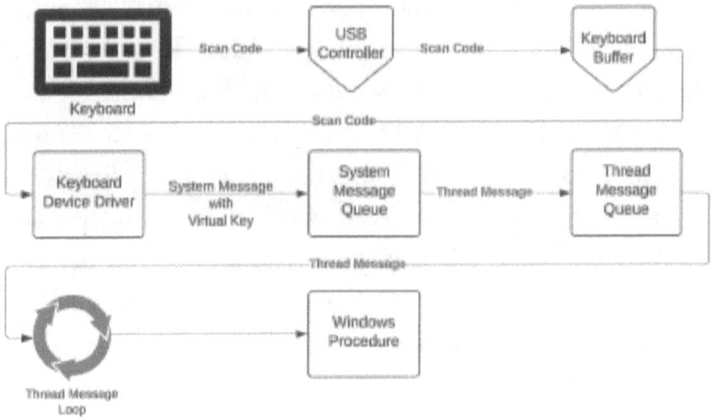

Figure II.1: Windows keyboard messaging

III
The Network

"Any sufficiently advanced technology is indistinguishable from magic."

– Arthur C. Clarke

And now a diversion into a discussion of networking before continuing the path of the "enter" key.

III.1
Physical Layer

AKA Layer 1.

The physical layer is the physical connection between devices. Standards govern the transmission of raw bit streams over physical mediums. Local wired networks are governed by the Ethernet standard (IEEE 802.3). Wireless local area networks are governed by Wi-Fi standard (IEEE 802.11). Bluetooth (IEEE 802.15.1) is for short range wireless communication. Fiber optic standards such as single mode optical fiber (ITU-T G.652).

Functions of the physical layer:

- **Bit Transmission**: Convert digital data into electrical, optical, or radio signals. Or vice versa.

- **Physical Medium**: Coaxial, twisted pair, fiber optic, wireless, etc.

- **Data Rate**: They physical layer specifies the data rate.

- **Synchronization**: Ensures the sender and receiver agree on when the bit starts and ends.

- **Line Configuration**: The configuration of the physical medium, whether it is point-to-point (direct link between devices) or multi-point.

- **Physical Topology**: Physical layout of the network. For example, star, ring, or mesh topologies.

- **Transmission Mode**: Whether the communication is simplex, half-duplex, or full duplex.

- **Signal Encoding**: How the data is encoded into signals for transmission. For example, modulation techniques for converting digital data into analog signals.

Components of the physical layer:

- **Network Interface Cards (NICs)**
- **Cables and Connectors**
- **Hubs and Repeaters**
- **Modems and Transceivers**

A signal on a network interface card:

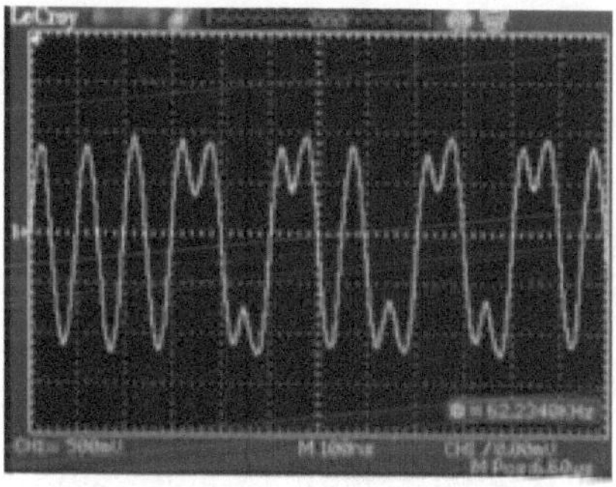

Figure III.1: Ethernet signal [9]

III.2
Data Link Layer

AKA Layer 2.

The data link layer is responsible for node-to-node data transfer and error detection and correction.

Functions of the data link layer:

- **Framing**: Dividing the raw bit stream into manageable chunks called frames. Adding a header and trailer to the payload (the data).

- **Addressing**: MAC addressing to identify each device on the same network segment.

- **Error Detection and Correction**: Uses techniques also identified in the physical layer.

- **Flow Control**: Manages the flow of data to prevent network congestion. An example is sliding window protocol to control the rate of data transmission.

- **Access Control**: Determines whether the device has a right to use the physical medium at any given time.

The data link layer is further divided into two sub-layers. The Logical Link Control (LLC) and the Media Access Control (MAC) sub-layers. LLC is responsible for error checking, flow control, and frame synchronization. While the MAC sub-layer is responsible for controlling access to the physical transmission medium. It handles addressing and channel access control mechanisms.

Common protocols in the data link layer are Ethernet, Wi-Fi, PPP (Point-to-Point)[2], HDLC (High-Level Data Link Control)[3].

III.3
Network Layer

AKA Layer 3.

The network layer is responsible for the ***logical*** addressing and routing of data packets across different networks. Functions of the network layer:

- **Logical Addressing**: This is typically referring to the IP addresses of devices on the network. They can be IPv4 which are 32-bit addresses (e.g.127.0.0.1) or IPv6 which are 128-bit addresses (e.g. 2001:0db8:85a3:0000:0000:8a2e:0370:7334).

- **Routing**: The network layer determines the best path for data packets to travel from the source to the destination. Routing selection involves algorithms that consider factors such as network topology, traffic load, and link costs. Common routing algorithms are Distance Vector Routing, Link State Routing, and Path Vector Routing.

- **Packet Forwarding**: The network layer uses routing tables to determine the next network to send the data packet.

- **Fragmentation and Reassembly**: If a packet is too large to send over a particular network segment, the network layer will further divide the packets into smaller pieces.

- **Error Handling and Diagnostics**: As with the previous layers, mechanisms are in place to handle errors, detect, and report the errors. This layer also provides many tools for network troubleshooting.

Common protocols used in the network layer:

- **Internet Protocol(IP)**: Most widely used protocol[4]used for the logical addressing and routing of packets based on their IP address.

- **Internet Control Message Protocol (ICMP)**: Used for error reporting and diagnostic functions, such as "ping" command to test connectivity.

- **Address Resolution Protocol (ARP)**: Maps IP addresses to MAC addresses, allowing devices to communicate within the same network segment.

- **Routing Protocols**: Protocols use to exchange routing information to determine the best paths for data packets. Examples are Open Shortest Path First (OSPF), Border Gateway Protocol (BGP), and Routing Information Protocol (RIP).

Physical (or sometimes virtual) devices that operate at the network layer:

- **Routers**: Can route data between different networks.

- **Switches**: Layer 3 switches can perform routing functions.

- **Firewalls**: Security devices that operate at the network layer to monitor and control incoming and outgoing network traffic based on predetermined security rules. See the security chapter for more details.

III.4 Transport Layer

AKA Layer 4.

While the network layer was responsible for routing, the transport layer is responsible for ensuring reliable data transfer.

Keep in mind that many of these functions look duplicated from the data link layer. They serve the same purpose but operate at a different scope. The transport layer ensures reliable communication between two hosts, which may or may not be on the same network segment. While the data link layer operates between two physical nodes. The data link layer can operate in a connectionless manner. In addition, the data link layer uses acknowledgments for each individual frame. This contrasts with the transport layer which acknowledges the highest sequence number receiver or in some cases uses Selective Acknowledgment (SACK) to acknowledge non-continuous data.

Another key difference is the "window" size for the flow control is usually fixed in the data link layer where the transport layer is dynamically adjusted based on congestion. Functions of the transport layer:

- **Segmentation and Reassembly**: Like the data link layer, large data streams are broken into smaller segments and then reassembled.

- **Connection Establishment and Termination**: Establishes, maintains, and terminates connections between devices.

- **Flow Control**: The sliding window protocol is used on this layer as well as congestion control mechanisms to prevent congestion. Common algorithms are slow start, congestion avoidance, and fast recovery.

- **Error Detection and Correction**: Similar techniques used on the data link layer are used here except the packets are examined between hosts.

- **Multiplexing and Demultiplexing**: The transport layer allows multiple applications to use the network simultaneously by assigning unique port numbers to each application. See the appendix for a list of well-known ports.

Key protocols of the transport layer:

- **Transmission Control Protocol (TCP)**: TCP is a

connection-oriented protocol that ensures data is delivered in the correct order without errors.

- **User Datagram Protocol (UDP)**: UDP is a connectionless protocol that uses best effort. No guarantees are made that the data is received in order or even received at all. UDP is used

when applications need low latency but can tolerate some data loss such as streaming and gaming.

TCP uses a three-way handshake to establish connection between the sender and receiver. This process involves:

- **SYN**: The sender sends a synchronization packet to the receiver.

- **SYN-ACK**: The receiver responds with a synchronization-acknowledgment packet.

- **ACK**: The sender sends an acknowledgment packet to confirm the connection.

TCP uses a four-step process to terminate a connection:

- **FIN**: Then sender sends a finish packet to the receiver.
- **ACK**: The receiver acknowledges the FIN packet.
- **FIN**: The receiver sends a FIN packet to the sender.
- **ACK**: The sender acknowledges the FIN packet, completing the termination.

Key components of the transport layer (note these are not physical devices):

- **Ports**: Logical endpoints to identify specific applications or services. Think of it as the address of the application within the transport layer.

- **Sockets**: The unique combination of IP address and Port defines the socket.

III.5
Session Layer

AKA Layer 5.

The session layer is responsible for establishing, managing, and terminating communication sessions between applications. For connectionless protocols like UDP, the session layer is typically not used. Functions of the session layer:

- **Session establishment, management, and termination**: When establishing the session, parameters such as the session identifier, session type (simplex, half-duplex, full-duplex), defining synchronization points within the data stream where synchronization should occur, timeout values for data transfer and session termination, error handling and correction, and flow control mechanisms are all defined. Other steps that take place in this step include authentication and authorization (which may include token exchanges), session negotiation, session establishment confirmation, and state management.

- **Dialog control**: This is the half or full duplex modes. Or simplex mode where each side takes a turn.

- **Synchronization**: The session layer implements synchronization points within the data stream. These points act as markers or checkpoints, allowing for efficient recovery from disruptions.

Key protocols of the session layer:

- **X.225 or ISO 8327**[8]

- **Zone Information Protocol (ZIP)**: AppleTalk protocol that coordinates the name binding process.[10]

- **Session Control Protocol (SCP)**: DECnet Phase IV protocol.[2]

Applications in the session layer include Remote Procedure Calls (RPCs) and Network File System file operations.

III.6
Presentation Layer

AKA Layer 6.

The presentation layer acts as a translator between the lower layers and the application layer. The function of translating includes converting date formats, changing the character encoding and data structures to ensure compatibility between different systems.

The presentation layer also handles data encryption and decryption to ensure sensitive information is protected during transmission.

Thepresentationlayerisalsoresponsibleforcompressinganddecompressing data to reduce the amount of data that needs to be transmitted.

And finally, the presentation layer converts complex data structures into a format that can be easily transmitted over the network. A process commonly known as serialization.

Key protocols and standards of the presentation layer:

- **ASCII (American Standard Code for Information Interchange)**: A character encoding standard used for text data.

- **EBCDIC (Extended Binary Coded Decimal Interchange Code)**: A character encoding standard primarily used on IBM mainframes.

- **JPEG (Joint Photographic Experts Group)**: A standard for compressing image data.

- **MPEG (Moving Picture Experts Group)**: A standard for compressing video and audio data.

- **TLS (Transport Layer Security)**: A protocol for encrypting data to ensure secure communication.

III.7
Application Layer

AKA Layer 7.

The application layer provides the interface between the application software and the underlying network. It provides network services to end-users and applications such as file transfer, email, remote login, and network management. The application layer defines the protocols that applications will use to communicate over the network such as HTTP (Hypertext Transfer Protocol), FTP (File Transfer Protocol), SMTP (Simple Mail Transfer Protocol), SNMP (Simple Network Management Protocol). It also provides services such as DNS (Domain Name System) and Telnet.

The application layer can ensure that the format of data is converted so it can be displayed to the end user. It also provides the user interfaces GUIs and CLIs (Graphical User Interfaces and Command Line Interfaces) to allow users to interact with network services.

III.8
Deep Dive

III.8.1 Synchronization

Clock signals between the sender and receiver are synchronized to ensure accurate data transfer. The receiver extracts the clock signal from the incoming data stream. This process is known as clock recovery. It involves using techniques like phase-locked loops to lock onto the timing of the incoming signal. Once the clock is recovered, the receiver can accurately determine the start and end of each bit. This ensures that the bits are sampled at the correct times, reducing the likelihood of errors.

Line encoding schemes such as Non-Return-to-Zero (NRZ), Manchester encoding, and 8b/10b encoding, are used to embed synchronization information within the data stream. Encoding schemes are designed to maintain a minimum transition density to help the receiver maintain synchronization. For example, Manchester encoding ensures that there is a transition in the middle of each bit period, making it easier to recover the clock signal.

Frame delimiters which include special start and stop bit patterns help the receiver identify the start and stop of frames.

Other techniques such as using parity bits[5], checksums[6], and cyclic redundancy checks (CRC)[7]are used to detect errors in the received data. If errors are detected, the receiver can request retransmission of the affected data.

III.8.2
Framing

Framing in the data link layer adds special bit patterns at the beginning and end of each frame to mark its boundaries. These patterns help the receiver identify where the frame starts and ends. Each frame contains the source and destination addresses. Frames also include error-detection codes like checksums or CRC. Frames are numbered to ensure that they are received in the correct order.

Character-Oriented framing (byte count with byte stuffing) uses special characters to delimit frames. While Bit-Oriented framing (bit count with bit stuffing) uses bit patterns to delimit frames. For example, HDLC uses 01111110 to mark the beginning and end of a frame.

The basic process of framing is receiving the data stream from the Network layer and then dividing the data into smaller chunks. The chunks are encapsulated with the header (addressing information), payload, and trailer (error-detection information). The boundaries of the frame are created. After transmission, the receiver extracts the payload after checking for errors.

It should be noted that with Fixed-Size framing (Byte-Count), there is no need for start and stop fields in the frame.

Flow Control

Flow control mechanisms:

1. **Stop-and-Wait**

• **Description**: The sender transmits a frame and waits for acknowledgment (ACK) from the receiver before sending the next frame.

• **Advantage**: Easy to implement.

• **Disadvantage**: Inefficient for high-speed networks.

2. **Sliding Window**

• **Description**: Sender transmits multiple frames before needing an ACK. The number of frames, "window", size determines when to send the ACK.

• **Advantage**: Allows continuous data transmission.

• **Disadvantage**: Requires more memory for buffering frames.

Some techniques used in framing are buffering where the sender and receiver store frames in memory to handle temporary communication speed changes. ACK's to confirm the receipt of data and NAK's (negative acknowledgments) to request a retransmission of data. Additionally, the receiver and request a size adjustment of the window to prevent congestion.

IV
The Request

"I normally don't do requests. Unless, of course, I have been asked to do so."

– Victor Borge

And the magic continues.

IV.1
URL Parsing

The first thing the browser does is parse the URL into its constituent parts. For example, consider the following query: "https://www.example.com/path/subpath?query=param"

- Protocol: https
- Domain: example.com
- Subdomain: www
- Path: /path/subpath
- Query Parameters: query=param

IV.2
DNS Resolution

The second thing the browser needs to do is translate the domain name into an IP address. The browser first checks its own DNS cache for the IP address. You can view what the browser has in its DNS cache. In Chrome and Edge browsers you can type:

"chrome://net-internals/#dns" to view the cache.

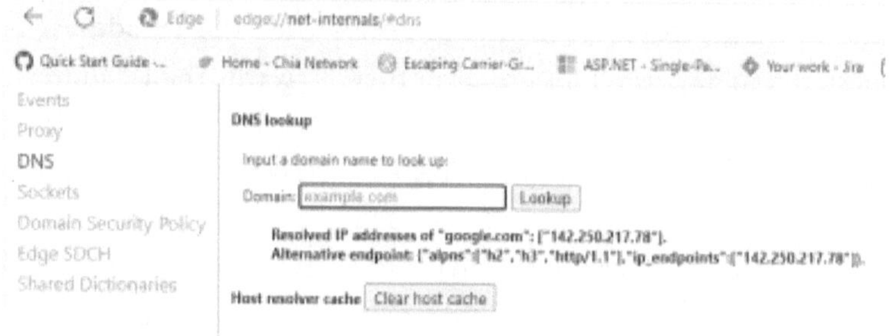

Figure IV.1: Browsing google.com DNS cache in an Edge browser

If the IP address is TTL (time-to-live) is expired, it sends the DNS query to the DNS server.

The Domain Name System (DNS) is a hierarchical and decentralized naming system used to translate human-readable domain names (like example.com) to IP addresses as explained in the networking chapter. The domain name is organized with a root level domain, represented by a dot(.). It contains root servers. Top-Level Domains (TLDs) include domains like .com, .org, .net, or country specific TLDs like .uk or .jp. Second-Level Domains are just below the TLDs. Such as google ingoogle.comorwhitehouseinwhitehouse.gov. Subdomains are below the second level domains like www in www.example.com or mysite in mysite.site.com.

Your computer, when configured on a network, is pre-configured with the IP address of a domain name server, usually provided by your ISP or network administrator. The browser sends a DNS query over port

53 (usually over UDP rather than TCP but there are exceptions) to the DNS server. The DNS server checks its own cache for the ip address, if found it responds and to the client and the request is over.

However, if the IP is not found the DNS resolver queries the root server for the TLD of the domain. The root server responds with the address of a TLD server responsible for the request TLD (e.g. .com). The DNS resolver then queries the TLD server, which responds with the address of the authoritative DNS server for the requested domain (e.g. example.com). And then finally, the DNS resolver queries the authoritative DNS server, which responds with the IP address of the requested domain. The DNS resolver then forwards the IP address back to the browser.

DNS servers store various types of records including:

- **A Record**: Maps domain name to IPv4 address

- **AAAA Record**: Maps a domain name to an IPv6 address

- **CNAME Record**: Maps a domain name to a another domain name (alias).

- **MX Record**: Specifies the mail servers for a domain.

- **TXT Record**: Stores text information for various purposes, such as SPF (Sender Policy Framework) records for email authentication.

DNS Security is crucial to prevent attacks like DNS spoofing and cache poisoning. Some security measures include DNS Security Extensions (DNSSEC) which adds cryptographic signatures to DNS records to ensure their authenticity and integrity.

IV.3 Establish a Connection

The Handshakes

For an HTTPS request, a secure connection is established using

TCP and TLS/SSL (Transport Layer Security/Secure Socket Layer) [8]using a handshake process and exchange of keys.

1. TCP Handshake as described in the Networking Chapter
2. TLS Handshake
    a. **Client Hello**: The client sends a "Client Hello" message to the server, which includes supported TLS versions, cipher suites, and a random number.
    b. **Server Hello**: The server responds with a "Server Hello" message, which includes the chosen TLS version, cipher suite, and another random number.
    c. **Server Certificate**: The server sends its digital certificate to the client for authentication. The digital certificate is a part of a chain of certificates ending with a trusted root certificate authority (CA)

• **Signature Verification**: The client verifies the digital signature on the certificate. This involves checking that the certificate was signed by a trusted CA. The client uses the public key of the CA to verify the signature.

• **Certificate Chain Validation**: The client validates the entire certificate chain, ensuring that each certificate in the chain is signed by a trusted CA. This process continues until the client reaches a trusted root CA.

• **Expiry Data**: The client checks the validity period of the server's certificate. It ensures that the certificate is not expired and is within the valid date range.

• **Revocation Status**: The client checks the revocation status of the server's certificate. This can be done using methods like Certificate Revocation Lists or the Online Certificate Status Protocol. The client ensures that the certificate has not be revoked by the CA.

• **Domain Name Matching**: The client verifies that the domain name in the server's certificate matches the domain name of the server it is connecting to. This ensures that the certificate is issued for the correct domain.

• **Trust Store**: The client maintains a trust store, which is a collection of trusted root CA certificates. The client checks that the root CA in the certificate is present in its trust store.

a. **Key Exchange**: The client and server exchange keys to establish a shared secret.
b. **Client Key Exchange**: The client generates a pre-master secret, encrypts it with the server's public key, and sends it to the server.
c. **Session Keys**: Both the client and server use the pre-master secret and random numbers to generate session keys for encryption.
d. **Finished Message**: Both the client and server send "Finished" messages to each other, encrypted with the session keys, to confirm the handshake.

After the TLS steps are taken, a secure channel is considered established.

IV.4
Build the Request

The browser then constructs the http request message which consists of the following components:

• **Request Line**: Specifies the HTTP method (PUT, POST, GET, OPTIONS, PATCH, TRACE, HEAD),

the path, and the HTTP version. For example: "GET

/path/subpath?query=param HTTP/2

• **Headers**: Include metadata about the request such as the host, user-agent, accept-language, and cookies.

• **Body**(Optional): Contains additional data to be sent to the server, typically used in a POST request.

IV.4.1 Request Line

The version number of the HTTP is included in the request line to ensure compatibility between features of the client and servers requests. Each version of HTTP defines specific behaviors and rules for how requests and responses should be handled. For example, HTTP/1.1 introduced persistent connections, chunked transfer encoding, and additional cache control mechanisms to HTTP/1.0.

HTTP/2 introduced binary format for data transmission making parsing more efficient and less error-prone. It also introduced multiplexing to allow multiple requests and responses to be sent simultaneously over a single TCP connection. HPACK header compression algorithm

was added to reduce the size of headers, especially for repeated headers. In HTTP/2, clients can change the priority levels of streams. Server push was also introduced allowing the server to push related files to the client such as CSS[9]and JavaScript[3] files. Other security features were added to HTTP/2.

RFC 2616 which specifies the HTTP/1.1 protocol and RFC 7450 which specifies the HTTP/2 protocol describe the various request methods, semantics and usage.

- **GET**: Retrieve data with NO side-effects.
- **POST**: Submit data to be processed. Causes a change or side effects on the server.
- **PUT**: Updates a resource.
- **DELETE**: Deletes a resource.

- **HEAD**: Similar to GET but only retrieve the headers.

- **OPTIONS**: Determines the capabilities of the server. Used in CORS[10]requests.

- **PATCH**: Modifies only a portion of a resource. For example, when sending a large file, patch requests are sent until the final

portion is sent.

- **TRACE**: Performs a message loop-back test for diagnostic purposes.

It should be noted that these are the definitions to how these request methods should be used. But there is nothing in place to enforce that a GET request will not modify the resource. It is the responsibility of the API developer to program to the standards.

IV.4.2
Headers

HTTP headers are key value pairs sent with both the request and the response. They provide essential information about the request or response, such as metadata, control data, and more.

Common request headers are:

- **Host**: Specifies the server host domain name and TCP port.

"Host: www.example.com". The host header is required by HTTP/1.1 even though the host is present on the request line.

This allows web servers that host multiple websites on the same IP address to understand which site to serve. It is also used by proxy servers[11]to determine which server to route the request.

- **User-Agent**: Provides information about the browser being used so the server can customize the response for differences in browsers.

- **Accept**: Specifies which media types the client will accept from the server (text, html, application, JavaScript, etc.)

- **Accept-Language**: Specifies the preferred response language.

- **Accept-Encoding**: Indicates the content encoding that the client can handle. gzip, deflate, br

- **Authorization**: Contains credentials for authenticating the client with the server

- **Cookie**: Sends cookies from the client to the server. Cookies are used for session management, personalization, and tracking. Common response headers are:

- **Content-Type**: Indicates the media type of the response content. This helps the client understand how to process the response body.

- **Content-Length**: Specifies the size of the response body in bytes. This helps the client know how much data to expect.

- **Set-Cookie**: Sends cookies from the server to the client.

- **Cache-Control**: Provides caching directives to specify how the response is cached by the client and intermediate proxies.

- **Expires**: Specifies the time and date after the response is determined to be stale. This helps the client determine how long to cache a response.

- **ETag**: Provides a unique identifier for a specific version of a resource. This helps the client determine if the resource has changed and if it needs to be re-fetched.

- **Location**: Indicates the URL to which the client should be redirected. This is used in redirection responses (301, 302).

Most security headers are set by the server. But the client can set the ORIGIN request header to prevent Cross-Site Request Forgery attacks. The REFERER header contains the URL of the previous web page from which a link to the currently requested page was followed. It helps in tracking the source of the request and can be used for security purposes.

Other common security headers sent in the response from the server are:

- **Content-Security-Policy**: Helps prevent cross-site scripting (XSS) attacks, clickjacking, and other code injection attacks by specifying which sources of content are allowed to be loaded.

- **Strict-Transport-Security**: Enforces the use of HTTPS for all communications with the server, preventing downgrade attacks and cookie hijacking.

- **X-Content-Type-Options**: Prevent the browser from interpreting files as a different MIME type than what is specified, which helps mitigate MIME type sniffing attacks.

- **X-Frame-Options**: Protects against clickjacking attacks by controlling whether the browser should allow the page to be displayed in a frame or iframe[12]

- **X-XSS-Protection**: Enables the browser's built-in XSS protection and instructs it on how to handle detected XSS attacks.

- **Referrer-Policy**: Controls how much referrer information is included with request made from your site, helping protect user privacy.

- **Permissions-Policy**: Controls which browser features can be used in web applications, such as geolocation, camera, and microphone.

IV.4.3
Body (Optional)

The body of an HTTP request or response can be in various formats, depending on the type of data transmitted and the requirements of the application. Here are some common formats:

- **Plain Text**: Hello, World!
- **HTML** (Hypertext Markup Language):

```
<html>
<head>

        <title>Example</title>

</head>
<body>

        <h1>Hello, World!</h1>

</body>
</html>
```

- **JSON** (JavaScript Object Notation):

```
{

        "name": "Dustin Morris",

"age": 50
}
```

- **XML** (eXtensible Markup Language):

```
<person>

        <name>Dustin Morris</name>
```

<age>50</age>

</person>

- **Form Data**: name=Dustin+Morris&age=50

- **Binary Data**: Quite literally, 1 and 0's for transmitting binary files, such as images, videos, and other non-text data.

- **Base64-Encoded Data**: Binary data encoded in Base64 for safe transmission over text-based protocols.

It should be noted that Base64 is not a form of encryption. It does not provide any security or confidentiality. It does, however, help with the Integrity portion of the CIA security triangle (Confidentiality, Integrity, and Availability). Base64 is actual just an encoding scheme that helps prevent data corruption that can occur in other character encodings. Base64 encoded data can be safely included in URLs, email bodies, and other text-based formats without causing issues with special characters or control characters. Although Base64 is not human readable, it is in a text format, making it easier to handle than raw binary data. Finally, Base64 helps prevent injection attacks that could exploit binary data in certain contexts, such as SQL injection or command injection.

IV.5
Send the Request

The following is the complete request through all 7 layers of the OSI Model. This text is converted into bits and bytes through the driver of the NIC(network interface card) and turned into electrical, wireless, or optical signals for transmission.

Ethernet Frame:

Destination MAC Address: 00:1A:2B:3C:4D:5E

Source MAC Address: 5E:4D:3C:2B:1A:00

EtherType: 0x0800 (IPv4)

Payload: (contains the IP packet)

IP Header:

Version: 4

Header Length: 20 bytes

Type of Service: 0

Total Length: 60 bytes

Identification: 0x1c46

Flags: 0x4000 (Don't Fragment)

Fragment Offset: 0

Time to Live (TTL): 64

Protocol: TCP (6)

Header Checksum: 0xb1e6

Source IP Address: 192.0.2.1

Destination IP Address: 203.0.113.1

TCP Header:

Source Port: 12345

Destination Port: 80

Sequence Number: 123456789

Acknowledgment Number: 987654321

Data Offset: 5

Flags: SYN, ACK
Window Size: 8192
Checksum: 0x1234
Urgent Pointer: 0
Options: (if any)
HTTP Request:
GET /path/to/resource HTTP/1.1
Host: www.example.com
User-Agent: Mozilla/5.0 (Windows NT 10.0; Win64; x64) AppleWebKit/537.36 (KHTML, like Gecko)

Chrome/87.0.4280.88 Safari/537.36

Accept: text/html,application/xhtml+xml, application/xml;q=0.9, image/webp,*/*;q=0.8

Accept-Language: en-US,en;q=0.9
Accept-Encoding: gzip, deflate, br Connection: keep-alive

IV.6
Deep Dive

IV.6.1
DNSSEC

DNSSEC uses digital signatures to verify the authenticity of DNS data. Each DNS zone has a pair of cryptographic keys: a public key and a private key. The private key is used to sign DNS records, and the public key is used to verify the signatures.

Two important records are the DNSKEY and RRSIG records. The DNSKEY contains the public key used to verify the signatures in the DNS zone. The RRSIG contains the digital signature for a set of DNS records. It is generated using the private key and is used to verify the integrity and authenticity of the DNS records.

The DNSSEC establishes a chain of trust from the root zone to the authoritative DNS servers for a domain. Each level in the DNS hierarchy signs its own records and includes the public key of the next level.

When the resolver receives a DNS response, it uses the public key in the DNSKEY record to verify the signature in the RRSIG record's digital signature. The resolver follows the chain of trust, verifying each level's signatures up to the root zone.

V
The Routing

"Navigation is a power of a limited sort – it enables us to manage the immensity of the media torrent."

– Todd Gitlin

And we are off to the races. Now the request is sent, it is up to the network routers to select the best path in the network to send the data packets. Routers segment networks and forward packets between segments. Routing information is stored in a routing table that the router uses to determine which segment to forward the request. The routing table contains information about the network topology and the next hop for each destination.

Destination Network	Subnet Mask	Next Hop	Interface	Metric
192.168.1.0	255.255.255.0	192.168.1.1	eth0	1
10.0.0.0	255.0.0.0	10.0.0.1	eth1	2
172.16.0.0	255.240.0.0	172.16.0.1	eth2	3
0.0.0.0	0.0.0.0	192.168.1.254	eth0	10

Table V.1: Example Routing Table

This example table shows the address of the destination network, the subnet mask for the destination network, the ip address of the next router in the hop, the physical interface in which the packet should be sent, and the cost of the route. If the destination is not explicitly listed in the table, a default route of 0.0.0.0 is used. 0.0.0.0 is the broadcast address.

Routing protocols are algorithms that determine the best path for data packets to travel across a network. They dynamically update the routing tables based on network topology changes. Common routing protocols are **RIP** (Routing Information Protocol) which uses hop count as a metric. **OSPF** (Open Shortest Path First) uses the link-state information to build a map of the network. **EIGRP** Enhanced Interior Gateway Routing Protocol is a Cisco proprietary protocol that combines the features of both distance-vector and link-state protocols. **BGP** (Border Gateway Protocol) is used for routing between different autonomous systems[13]. RIP, OSPF, and EIGRP are known as Interior Gateway Protocols(IGPs) that are designed to communicate within a single autonomous system. While BGP is an Exterior Gateway Protocol (EGP) designed for communication between systems.

OSPF uses packets called Link-State Advertisements (LSAs) that contain information about the interfaces (links) and the routers connected to them. Types of LSAs include:

- **Router LSA (Type 1)**: Contains information about the router's interfaces and their states.

- **Network LSA (Type 2)**: Contains information about the routers connected to a specific network segment.

- **Summary LSA (Type 3 and 4)**: Contains information about routes to networks outside of the local area.

- **AS External LSA (Type 5)**: Contains information about routes to external autonomous systems.

A Link-State Database (LSDB) is maintained in routers that use the OSPF protocol. It stores the LSAs received from other routers. OSPF routers routinely synchronize their LSDBs to ensure they have a consistent view of the network.

OSPF uses the Dijkstra algorithm, also known as the Shortest Path First (SPF) algorithm, to calculate the shortest path to each destination based on the link-state information in the LDSB. The SPF builds the shortest-path tree with the router as the root and calculates the shortest path to each destination.

OSPF networks can be divided into areas to optimize routing and reduce the size of the LSDB. The backbone area (Area 0) is the central area that connects all other areas in an OSPF network. All inter-area traffic must pass through the backbone area.

Where OSPF is used within a single autonomous system (AS), BGP is used between organizations. Each AS is assigned a unique identifier

(ASN). Routers in different ASes establish a TCP connection on port 179 to exchange routing information. A BGP route advertisement consists of a block of IP addresses that a router advertises to its BGP peers. It contains path attributes associated with the route. The advertisement also contains a list of ASes that a route has traversed to prevent routing loops. The BGP uses several steps in the decision process to select the best path to a destination:

1. **Highest Local Preference**: Prefers routes with the highest local preference value.
2. **Shortest AS Path**: Prefers routes with the shortest AS path.
3. **Lowest Origin Type**: Prefers routes with the lowest origin type (IGP<EGP<Incomplete)
4. **Lowest Multi-Exit Discriminator (MED**: Prefers the routes with the lowest MED[14]value.
5. **eBGP over iBGP**: Prefers routes learned via eBGP over iBGP.
6. **Lowest IGP Metric**: Prefers routes with the lowest IGP metric to the next hop.
7. **Oldest Route**: Prefers the oldest route if all other factors are equal.
8. **Lowest Router ID**: Prefers routes from the router with the lowest router ID.

VI
The Server

"I did not have textual relations with that server."
– Hillary Clinton bumper sticker (author unknown)

And the message is received near the destination. But first it usually must go through a couple of steps before the application server takes action. The first hurdle is filtering through a Web Application Firewall (WAF). The second step is through a reverse proxy server, also known as a load balancer.

The WAF inspects traffic by analyzing the http requests and filtering based on pre-defined rules. The WAF inspects headers, URLs, cookies, and payloads. WAFs use predefined rules to identify common attack patterns, such as SQL injection, cross-site scripting, and remote file inclusion. WAFs also use signature-based detection by looking for attack signatures that match known exploits or vulnerabilities. A signature database is regularly updated to include new threats and attack vectors. Some advanced WAFs use behavioral analysis and machine learning to dynamically adapt to problems. Such as unusual request rates, unexpected parameter values, or other abnormal user behavior. They also perform functions such as checking for malformed requests, invalid headers, and other protocol violations. When WAFs detect abnormalities, they can be configured to block the request and alert a central notification system (commonly a Security Information and Event Management System (SEIM).

After passing inspection, the packet is forwarded to the load-balancer. The IP address the client communicates with is more than likely the load-balancer. Like the WAF, the load-balancer can be dedicated hardware or software defined. The purpose of the load-balancer is to distribute network traffic across multiple servers to ensure optimal resource utilization, high availability, and reliability. It uses various algorithms to determine how to distribute traffic. Common algorithms used are:

- **Round Robin**: Each server in a server pool receives traffic in sequential order.

- **Least Connections**: Sends traffic to the server with the fewest active connections.

- **IP Hash**: Uses the client's IP address to determine wich server will handle the request.

- **Weighted Round Robin**: Assigns weights to servers based on their capacity, distributing accordingly.

- **Least Response Time**: Directs traffic to the server with the fastest response time.

Load balancers perform regular health checks on servers to ensure they are available and function correctly. Although HTTP requests themselves are stateless, some scenarios such as large file transfers require multiple requests during one session. To ensure the same server that instantiated the session receives the traffic, a sticky session is created by the load balancer, known as session persistence. Session persistence can be achieved using cookies, IP addresses, or other identifiers.

One important task of many load balancers is SSL/TLS offloading. The load balancer will handle the handshake, removing the load from the busier servers. This also simplifies SSL certificate management because only the load balancer(s) need a certificate.

Load balancing enables horizontal scaling by adding more servers to the pool as demand increases. They also provide redundancy by distributing traffic across multiple servers, if one server fails, others can take the load.

There are many things that happen on the server end, depending on the use case. I will leave the details for another book. But here is a summary of topics that might be discussed:

- **Databases**
- **Key-Value Stores**
- **Content Delivery Networks**
- **Sequencers**
- **Rate Limiters**
- **Distributed Search**
- **Distributed Logging**
- **Distributed Scheduling**
- **Blob stores**

For now, it is important to know that the server is just an application running on another computer listening on a predefined port for the request on the network. The request is received through the network interface card, through the operating system and kernel drivers, up to the server application. The server does some magic of its own (programmed by the application developer) and then crafts the response in a similar manner to how the client crafted the request.

One important feature of the response is the response status code. You may be familiar with the 404-status code when a client sends a bad request. Often indicated by fun bad response status pages or directions on how to correct the problem.

Other status codes fall into one of five groups. Some common status codes are:

1.XX **Informational**:

- **100 Continue**: The server has received the request headers, and the client should proceed to send the request body.

• **101 Switching Protocols**: The server is switching protocols as requested by the client.

2.XX **Successful**

200 OK: The request was successful, and the server has returned the requested resource.

• **201 Created**: The request was successful, and a new resource was created.

• **204 No Content**: The request was successful, but there is no content to send in the response.

3.XX **Redirection**:

• **301 Moved Permanently**: The requested resource has been permanently moved to a new URL.

• **302 Found**: The requested resource is temporarily available at a different URL.

• **304 Not Modified**: The requested resource has not been modified since the last request.

4.XX **Client Error**

• **400 Bad Request**: The server could not understand the request due to invalid syntax.

• **401 Unauthorized**: The client must authenticate itself to get the requested response.

• **403 Forbidden**: The client does not have permission to access the requested resource.

- **404 Not Found**: The server cannot find the requested resource.

5.XX **Server Error**

- **500 Internal Server Error**: The server encountered an unexpected condition that prevented it from fulfilling the request.

- **502 Bad Gateway**: The server received an invalid response from an upstream server.

- **503 Service Unavailable**: The server is currently unable to handle the request due to temporary overload or maintenance.

VII
The Security

"In the old days, people robbed stagecoaches and knocked off armored trucks. Now they're knocking off servers."

– Richard Power

And the request should be sent to the server with confidentiality and integrity. The server and network should be available to receive the request. Confidentiality of the request implies that only the sender and receiver have knowledge of the payload contents. Integrity implies that the sender (the client) is actually the one who sent the message and not some middleman interloper or spoofer. Availability means that an attack does not significantly slow down communications between the sender and receiver. These three functions, CIA, form the security triangle.

Cybersecurity is a huge topic, but I will try and cover an overview with a few details here. Let's first look at each layer of the OSI model and how it can be attacked at each layer. We will also look at the countermeasures usually taken.

1. **Physical Layer Attacks**:

- **Physical Tampering**: Unauthorized access to physical network components.

Eavesdropping: Intercepting communication signals.
- **Cable Interference**: Cutting or tapping into network cables.

Countermeasures:

- **Physical Security**: Secure access to network equipment and cables.
- **Encryption**: Encrypt data to prevent eavesdropping.

• **Environmental Controls**: Protect against water or dust.

2. **Data Link Layer Attacks**:

• **MAC Spoofing**: Changing the MAC address to impersonate another device.

• **ARP Spoofing**: Sending fake ARP messages to associate the attacker's MAC address with a legitimate IP address.

Countermeasures:

• **Port Security**: Restrict access to network ports based on MAC addresses.

• **Dynamic ARP Inspection (DAI)**: Validate ARP packets to prevent spoofing.

• **VLAN Segmentation**: Isolate network segments to limit the impact of attacks.

3. **Network Layer Attacks**:

• **IP Spoofing**: Sneding packets with a forged IP address.
• **Routing Attacks**: Manipulating routing information to redirect traffic.

Countermeasures:

• **Access Control Lists (ACLs)**: Filter traffic based on IP addresses.
• **Secure Routing Protocols**: Use protocols like OSPF with authentication.
• **IPsec**: Encrypt and authenticate IP packets.

4. **Transport Layer Attacks:**

- **SYN Flood:** Overwhelming a server with SYN requests to exhaust resources.
- **Port Scanning:** Scanning for open ports to identify vulnerable services.

Countermeasures:

- **Rate Limiting:** Limit the number of connections to a single source.

- **Firewalls:** Block unauthorized access to ports.

- **Intrusion Detection System (IDS):** Monitor and detect suspicious activities.

5. **Session Layer Attacks:**

- **Session Hijacking:** Taking over an active session by stealing session tokens.

- **Session Fixation:** Forcing a user to use a known session ID.

Countermeasures:

- **Session Encryption:** Encrypt session data to prevent hijacking.
- **Session Timeouts:** Automatically terminate active sessions.
Token Validation: Use secure tokens and validate them on the server side.

6. **Presentation Layer Attacks:**

- **Phishing:** Trick users into providing sensitive information.

- **Man-in-the-Middle (MitM)**: Intercept and alter data between two parties.

Countermeasures:

- **SSL/TLS**: Encrypt data to prevent MitM attacks.
- **Data Validation**: Validate and sanitize data before processing.
- **User Education**: Train users to recognize phishing attempts.

7. **Application Layer Attacks**:

- **SQL Injection**: Injecting malicious SQL queries to manipulate databases.

- **Cross-Site Scripting (XSS)**: Injecting malicious scripts into web pages.

- **Cross-Site Request Forgery (CSRF)**: Target web applications by tricking user into performing actions they did not intend to perform.

Countermeasures:

- **Input Validation**: Validate and sanitize user inputs.

- **Web Application Firewalls (WAF)**: Filter and monitor HTTP traffic.

- **Secure Coding Practices**: Follow best practices for secure application development.

• • • •

VII.0.1
Cross Site Request Forgery

The way CSRF works is an authenticated victim unknowingly executes code embedded in a link from a DIFFERENT website controlled by the attacker. When this link is clicked, a carefully crafted request causes the server to execute an unintended action (like transfer money from your bank account into the attackers account). The server sees the action as coming from a legitimate authenticated user.

Countermeasures for CSRF include adding unique tokens to forms and urls that must be validated by the server (Anti-CSRF Tokens). Restrict access to cookies with the SameSite attribute. Check the referer header to validate the request originated from the same site. And finally requiring user interactions for sensitive actions (like CAPTCHA).

Another security feature implemented by the client's own web browser that an API programmer can use to help its clients is by using Cross-Origin Resource Sharing (CORS). This allows the API programmer to specify exactly which URLs are allowed to make requests.

VII.0.2 Cross Origin Resource Sharing

CORS utilizes various headers and a preflight mechanism to validate whether a request can be made from a different site than the original

site (samesite). Common headers used in CORS requests are:

- **Request Headers**

– **Origin**: Indicates the origin (scheme, host, and port) of the request. The server uses this header to determine whether to allow the request.

– **Access-Control-Request-Method**: Specifies the HTTP method (e.g., GET, POST, PUT) that will be used in the actual request.

– **Access-Control-Request-Headers**: Lists the headers that will be included in the actual request.

- **Response Headers:**

• **Access-Control-Allow-Origin**: Specifies which origins are allowed to access the resource. For example, "*" allows all origins,

while "https://example.com" allows only the specified origin.

• **Access-Control-Allow-Methods**: Lists the HTTP methods (e.g., GET, POST, PUT) that are allowed when accessing the resource.

• **Access-Control-Allow-Headers**: Specifies which headers can be used in the actual request. For example, "Content-Type, Authorization".

• **Access-Control-Allow-Credentials**: Indicates whether the response to the request can be exposed when the flag is true.

• **Access-Control-Expose-Headers**: Lists the headers that are safe to expose to the API of a CORS API specification.

• **Access-Control-Max-Age**: Indicates how long the results of a preflight request can be cached. Forexample,"86400" (24 hours). • Response Headers

– **Access-Control-Request-Method**: Used in preflight requests to let the server know which HTTP method will be used in the actual request.

– **Access-Control-Request-Headers**: Used in preflight requests to let the server know which HTTP headers will be used in the actual request.

For some requests, browsers send a preflight request using the OPTIONS method to ask the server if the actual request is allowed.

The preflight request includes the request headers specified above and server responds with ACCESS-CONTROL-(ALLOW-ORIGIN, ALLOWMETHODS, ALLOW-HEADERS, MAX-AGE). The client then responds with the actual request if allowed by the server's response.

VII.0.3
Secure Coding Practices

Secure coding practices is a singular umbrella term for a multitude of best practices.

SCPs include input validation. This means ensure that the input received is in the expected form. It also means sanitizing the inputs to prevent injection attacks like SQL injection or cross-site scripting. Sanitizing usually involves parsing the input to find control characters and sequences that shouldn't be present in the user's input data. Input validation in some cases may have an "allowed" list to validate inputs against a set of allowed values.

SCPs includes authentication and authorization. Is the user who they say they are(authentication)? Is the user authorized to use or access this resource (authorization)? Secure coding practices enforce strong passwords and use multi-factor authentication. Role-Based Access Control (RBAC) is one way and a very strong way of making sure users only have the necessary permissions necessary.

SCPs include data protection. This includes encrypting data in transit by enforcing secure protocols and encrypting data at rest. The encryption algorithm chosen is important. For example, MD5 encryption is known to be exploitable. Encryption should use algorithms such as SHA256 or SHA512. Developers should not check in secrets into repositories nor use hard-coded credentials.

SCPs include proper error handling. Errors should be handled gracefully without exposing sensitive information. For example, buffer overflows and underflows should be accounted for when managing memory. Potential null values should always be checked. Logs should provide a balance between providing necessary troubleshooting details and audit information with protecting sensitive data including customer's business data, personally identifiable information, or secrets.

SCPs include using secure communications. SSL/TLS communication between clients and servers. Properly manage and update SSL/TLS certificates.

SCPs include code review and testing. All code checked in should be reviewed for security flaws by peers. Tools should be used to conduct static and dynamic analysis of vulnerabilities every time code is checked in. Regular penetration testing will help identify and address security weaknesses.

SCPs include the Secure Development Lifecycle (SDLC). At the beginning of the development process, security requirements are defined. Threat modeling is used to identify potential threats and design countermeasures. Regular security training of developers to ensure they are aware of best practices are important.

SCPs include using a secure configuration. This involves avoiding default settings and credentials in production environments. Configuration management to have consistent and secure configuration.

SCPs include monitoring and incident response. As a developer, you should know when your software is compromised before your customer does. Proper monitoring with an incident response plan in place before the breach occurs. The incident response plan should define the roles and responsibilities for team members. A communication plan for the stakeholders both internal and external. All the tools for monitoring and responding should be in place and available. The incident response plan should include detection methods and classification. It should include containment procedures. Both short term to limit the impact and long term strategies to prevent further damage. The incident response should include a root cause analysis and removal of malicious artifacts such as malware, unauthorized access, etc. The plan should include a system restoration plan, data recovery plan, and validation plan to ensure the systems are functioning correctly and securely.

Cybersecurity is a topic of its own. And best left for a book on its own. However, as a primer the reader should review the Open Worldwide Application Security Project (OWASP) website as reference in the bibliography.[7]

VIII
Appendix

VIII.1
Well-Known Ports by Name

BGP (Border Gateway Protocol): Port 179

- **DNS (Domain Name System)**: Port 53
- **FTP (File Transfer Protocol)**: Ports 20 and 21
- **HTTP (Hypertext Transfer Protocol)**: Port 80
- **HTTPS (HTTP Secure)**: Port 443
- **IMAP (Internet Message Access Protocol)**: Port 143
- **IMAPS (IMAP over SSL/TLS)**: Port 993
- **IRC (Internet Relay Chat)**: Ports 194 and 6667
- **Kerberos**: Port 88
- **LDAP (Lightweight Directory Access Protocol)**: Port 389
- **MySQL**: Port 3306
- **MSSQL**: Port 1433
- **NTP (Network Time Protocol)**: Port 123
- **Oracle DB**: Port 1521
- **POP3 (Post Office Protocol version 3)**: Port 110
- **POP3S (POP3 over SSL/TLS)**: Port 995
- **PostgreSQL**: Port 5432
- **RDP (Remote Desktop Protocol)**: Port 3389
- **SMTP (Simple Mail Transfer Protocol)**: Port 25
- **SMTPS (SMTP over SSL/TLS)**: Port 465
- **SNMP (Simple Network Management Protocol)**: Ports 161 and 162
- **SSH (Secure Shell)**: Port 22
- **Syslog**: Port 514
- **Telnet**: Port 23
- **TFTP (Trivial File Transfer Protocol)**: Port 69

VIII.2
Well-Known Ports by Number

20 & 21: FTP (File Transfer Protocol)

- **22**: SSH (Secure Shell)
- **23**: Telnet
- **25**: SMTP (Simple Mail Transfer Protocol)
- **53**: DNS (Domain Name System)
- **69**: TFTP (Trivial File Transfer Protocol)
- **80**: HTTP (Hypertext Transfer Protocol)
- **88**: Kerberos
- **110**: POP3 (Post Office Protocol)
- **123**: NTP (Network Time Protocol)
- **143**: IMAP (Interment Message Access Protocol)
- **161 & 162**: SNMP (Simple Network Management Protocol
- **179**: BGP (Border Gateway Protocol)
- **194**: & 6667 IRC (Internet Relay Chat)
- **389**: LDAP (Lightweight Directory Access Protocol)
- **443**: HTTPS (HTTP Secure)
- **465**: SMPTPS (SMTP over SSL/TLS)
- **514**: Syslog
- **993**: IMAPS (IMAP over SSL/TLS)
- **995**: POP3S (POP3 over SSL/TLS)
- **1433**: MSSQL
- **1521**: Oracle DB
- **3306**: MySQL
- **3389**: RDP (Remote Desktop Protocol)
- **5432**: PostgresSQL

VIII.3
Common HTTP Headers[1]

- **Accept**:

  – **Accept**: Request and Response. Which content types the sender is able to understand. Browsers use the MIMI type and not the file extension. MIME types are expressed as type/subtype and defined by IETF's RFC 6838 standard.

  – **Accept-CH**: Response. Provide hints to client settings like viewport width and memory.

  – **Accept-Encoding**: Request and Response. Type of content the sender understands. The server uses content negotiation to select one of the encoding proposals.

  – **Accept-Language**: Request. Users preferred natural language. Maybe a list with quality factors.

  – **Accept-Patch**: Response. Which media types the server can accept patch requests for.

  – **Accept-Post**: Response. Which media types the server can accept post requests for.

  – **Accept-Ranges**: Response. Tells client whether server can accept request ranges for a portion of the resource.

• • • •

- **Access-Control**:

– **Access-Control-Allow-Credentials**: Response. Whether the server allows credentials to be including in cross-origin HTTP requests.

– **Access-Control-Allow-Headers**: Response. Used in preflight request to specify which headers are allowed in the request. Note: CORS-safe listed request headers are usually not listed here.

– **Access-Control-Allow-Methods**: Response. Allowed HTTP methods on request.

– **Access-Control-Allow-Origin**: Response. Whether the requesting code from an origin can access a resource.

– **Access-Control-Expose-Headers**: Response. Specifies which non-CORS listed safe headers can be accessed by browser scripts.

– **Access-Control-Max-Age**: Response. How long the results of the preflight request can be cached.

– **Access-Control-Request-Headers**: Request. Used in preflight request to let the server know which headers the client might send.

– **Access-Control-Request-Method**: Request. Used in preflight request to let the server know which method will be used.

• **Age**: Response. Lets the client know how long an object was in a proxy cache.

• **Allow**: Response. Sent with 405 (Method Not Allowed) with a list of allowed methods.

- **Authorization**: Request. Used to provide credentials.
- **Cache-Control**: Request and Response. Instructions on how to cache.
- **Clear-Site-Data**: Response. Signals client to clear cookies, storage, or cache.
- **Content-Encoding**: Lists the encodings and order they were applied to the resource. Lets the recipient know how to decode.
- **Content-Length**: Lists the size, in bytes, of the message body.
- **Content-Security-Policy**: Response. Controls the resources the user agent is allowed to load for a given page.
- **Content-Type**: Indicates the original media type of a resource before any content encoding is applied.
- **ETag**: Response. A unique identifier for a specific version of a resource. Helps caches be more efficient and helps prevent simultaneous updates of a resource.
- **Forwarded**: Request. Information the may be added by reverse proxy servers thout would otherwise be altered or lost when proxy servers are involved in the path of the request.
- **Host**: Request. Specifies the host and port number of the server to which the request is being sent.
- **If**: If requests make a request conditional.

  – **If-Match**: Request. If the ETag matches.
  – **If-Modified-Since**
  – **If-None-Match**: Request. If no ETag matches.
  – **If-Range** – **If-Unmodified-Since**

- **Last-Modified**: Response. When the server believes the resource was last modified.
- **Location**: Response. Indicates the URL to redirect to.
- **Origin**: Request. The scheme://hostname:port used to cause the request.

- **Proxy-Authenticate**: Response. Defines the authentication method the request should use to gain access to a resource behind a proxy server. Sent went 407 Proxy Authentication Required
- **Proxy-Authorization**: Request. Credentials to authenticate with the proxy server.
- **Range**: Request. The part of the resource the server should return.
- **Refresh**: Response. Directs the browser to refresh or redirect the page when a specified amount of time has passed since the page was fully loaded.
- **Set-Cookie**: Response. Send a cookie from the server to the user agent so it can be sent back to the server at a later time.
- **Strict-Transport-Security**: Response. Requires browsers to use HTTPS and can not downgrade to HTTP.
- **User-Agent**: Request. Lets the servers know what application, operating system, vendor, and/or version of the requesting user agent. product/product-version comment
- **Via**: Request and Response. Added by proxies to track message forwards and avoid request loops.
- **WWW-Authenticate**: Response. Used to list the types of authentication schemes that may be used.
- **X-Content-Type-Options**: Response. Indicates that the content-type headers should be respected and not changed. The header allows you to avoid MIME type sniffing.

VIII.4
MIME Types

Mime types are in one of 11 registries. https://www.iana.org lists all of the registered mime types.[6]

- **application**
- **audio**
- **example**
- **font**
- **haptics**
- textbfimage
- **message**
- **model**
- **multipart**
- **text**
- **video**

Examples are: application/pdf, application/vc+json, audio/mp4, audio/mpeg, font/ttf, font/woff, haptics/ivs/ image/apng, image/bmp, model/vrml, model/stl, multipart/mixed, multipart/voice-message, text/calendar, text/plain, video/3gpp, video/JPEG.

IX Bibliography

1. *Accept - HTTP | MDN.* https://developer.mozilla. org/en-US/ docs/Web/HTTP/Headers/Accept. Accessed: 2025-01-08. 2025.
2. *DECnet - Wikipedia.* https://en.wikipedia.org/wiki/ DECnet. Accessed: 2025-01-03. 2025.
3. *How do computer keyboards work?* https://www.youtube. com/ watch?v=h-NM1xSSzHQ. Accessed: 2025-01-02. 2023.
4. Karl-Bridge-Microsoft. *Keyboard Input Overview - Win32 apps*

| Microsoft Learn. https://learn.microsoft.com/enus/windows/win32/ inputdev/about-keyboard-input.

Accessed: 2025-01-02. 2025.

1. *Keyboard controller (computing) - Wikipedia.* https : / / en.wikipedia.org/wiki/Keyboard_controller_

(computing). Accessed: 2025-01-02. 2025.

1. *Media Types.* https://www.iana.org/assignments/ media-types/ media-types.xhtml. Accessed: 2025-01-08. 2025.
2. *OWASP Top Ten | OWASP Foundation.* https://owasp. org/ www-project-top-ten/. Accessed: 2025-01-07. 2025.
3. tsbmail. *X.22A:A Information technology Open Systems Interconnection Connection-oriented Session protocol: Protocol specification.* https://www.itu.int/rec/T-REC-X.225-199511-

I/en. Accessed: 2025-01-03. 2025.

1. *what does the eletrical signal look like on an ethernet cable Search.*

https://www.bing.com/videos/riverview/ relatedvideo ? q = what + does + the + eletrical + signal+look+like+on+an+ethernet+cable&mid= FD291417C8DFEA9D766FFD291417C8DFEA9D766F & mmscn = serpvidol & mcid =

E79B3E0D3A594E7CBCC71EAE85FD572A&FORM=VIRE& ajaxhist=0&ajaxserp=0. Accessed: 2025-01-05. 2025. [10] *Zone Information Protocol.* https://developer.apple. com/library/archive/documentation/mac/pdf/

Networking/ZIP.pdf. Accessed: 2025-01-03. 2025.

---

[1] A kernel-mode driver is a type of software that operates at a low level with the operating system and has direct access to the hardware and system resources.

[2] A protocol used for direct communications. Often used in dial-up communications.

[3] A bit-orientedprotocolusedforpoint to-pointandmultipointcommunication.

[4] A protocol is a set of rules and conventions that govern the communication between devices in a network.

[5] Even parity ensures that the total number of 1 bits is even. Conversely, odd parity ensures that the total number of 1 bits are odd.

[6] Before the data is transmitted, a checksum is calculated and sent with the data. It is then verified by the receiver.

[7] The data is divided by a predefined Generator Polynomial (ex. 1011) and the result of that division is the CRC value appended to the original data.

[8] SSL is the predecessor to TLS but they are commonly referred to together.

[9] CSS-Cascading Style Sheets control the look of web pages [3]JavaScript is a programming language used in browsers.

[10] See the security chapter for a discussion on CORS.

[11] A proxy server, or more than likely a reverse proxy server, provides a consistent path for the client to connect but will route the request to one of many different servers depending on configuration settings.

[12] a frame or iframe in this case is a separate place on the webpage defined by the <iframe> html tag which allows loading a different source of html within the current html document.

[13] Autonomous systems are a collection OSPF networks under the control of a single organization.

[14] MED is an integer value set by routing policies or manually by the network administrator.

www.ingramcontent.com/pod-product-compliance
Lightning Source LLC
LaVergne TN
LVHW090428210926
848480LV00002B/739
* 9 7 9 8 2 3 0 0 1 0 8 4 5 *